This book belongs to:

____

____

____

James was a quiet little boy at school. He listened to his teachers and raised his hand to answer questions enthusiastically. He was happy when the teachers said he was a 'good boy!' or said ' yes, that answer is correct- well done!'

James also enjoyed playtime activities and taking part in hobbies regularly. He joined clubs like football, Irish dancing and karate. At church, he joined the Adventurers and Pathfinders clubs and went on camping trips to lots and lots of different countries!

When he was practising his hobbies at home,
he would do some of his karate moves in
the kitchen and play his instruments in his
bedroom. He wanted to be good at everything
he tried. All of his teachers were a huge
inspiration, he want to be just as good as they
were!

James' Mummy worked as a doctor, he saw her working hard to help patients, giving them information on how they can get better. James liked to see how people reacted when his Mummy spoke to them. He was a little afraid of seeing blood, but he knew the patients were happy and relieved when they got better.

9

James would sometimes play with his
Mummy's stethoscope and auriscope. He used
the stethoscope to listen to his own heartbeat
and the auriscope to look into his brother's
ears. He liked turning on the light to see what
was down there. It made his brother laugh as
it tickled him!

When he was 11, James started secondary school. His new favourite subjects were biology, chemistry and physics. All of his teachers realised that James was very hard-working. They encouraged him to carry on playing music and to participate in sports as well as doing well in class.

13

James was a confident boy and if there was a school play or an orchestral performance, he would be brave enough to perform a solo in front of an audience. He was happy to show off his talents in front of other pupils, parents and even at church!

When James was 13 years old, it was time to choose subjects for his General Certificates of Secondary Education (GCSEs) at school. James wanted to be a doctor, just like his Mummy and so he chose to study biology, chemistry and physics as well as German and Latin. He worked very hard and at the end of his examinations, he gained fantastic grades!

When he was 16 he had to study for the International Baccalaureate. This is a series of six examinations taken by pupils all around the world. Again, James chose mainly science subjects.

Guten Tag!
salve!
GCSE

The subjects were difficult and at times James wasn't sure if he wanted to be a doctor! His careers advisor told him that he might be better at being a psychologist, but James really wanted to be a medical doctor after all just like his Mummy.

He started to think of all the things he could do...

MEDICINE
PSYCHOLOGY

For those people who had more serious illnesses, James could help them with medication or undertake operations to remove diseased tissues from their bodies.

He could help ladies to have their babies, help people with kidney disease or skin problems. He could also help those people who may have joint problems and who may not be able to walk very far.

Being a doctor would give James so many different opportunities to help people.

21

Soon, James applied to medical school. There was a long wait before he got the news that he had been offered a place at one of the top London universities if he received good results on his examinations.

The hope of going to University made him work hard in his International Baccalaureate subjects.

James took his International Baccalaureate
and he got the results that the University
said he needed. He said goodbye to all of his
friends and family and went down to London
where he studied for 6 years. He kept in touch
with his old friends and he made many new
ones.

James knew that when he finished medical school he would be a diligent doctor.

He was glad because he had made the right choices and he would be able to help lots of sick people in the future!

If you work hard, you could be a diligent doctor like James!

If you want to be a diligent doctor, take a look at these references to learn how!

For Kids:

Fun Kids Live
Fun Kids Live Doctors and GP's page explaining the roles and careers of various doctors as well as the path to medicine.
www.funkidslive.com/learn/homeschool/all-about-medicine/mission-1-doctors-and-gps/

Fun Kids Live
Fun Kids Live All About Medicine page with various links to pages surrounding the medical field.
https://www.funkidslive.com/learn/homeschool/all-about-medicine/

Kids Britannica
Kids Britannica page explaining the role of a doctor and route to medicine.
www.kids.britannica.com/kids/article/doctor/611075

For parents and guardians:

National Careers
National careers service summary of essential aspects of being a doctor.
https://nationalcareers.service.gov.uk/job-profiles/hospital-doctor

General Medical Council
Guidance on how to become a medical doctor in the UK as well as
relevant links to access more information from the British Medical
Council and other medical associations.
https://www.gmc-uk.org/education/becoming-a-doctor-in-the-uk

UCAS
Universities and Colleges Admissions Service (UCAS) guidance on
courses related to medicine as well as the entry requirements to get into
University and finance options for students.
https://www.ucas.com/explore/subjects/medicine-and-allied-subjects

What do you want to be when you grow up? Draw it below!

Notes!

Check out some other books in the series!

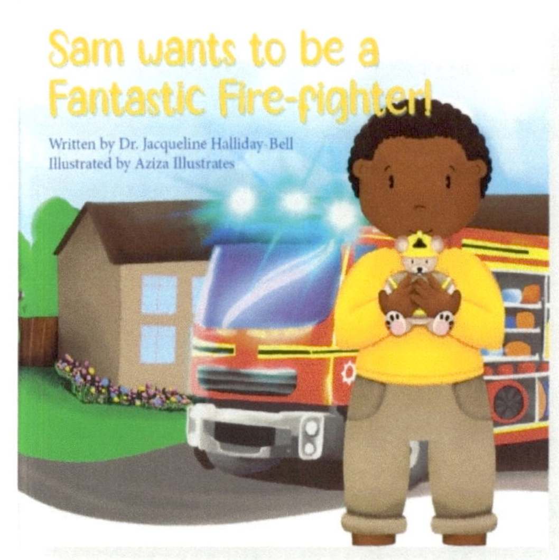